MARGARET THATCHER

A Not-Too-Tall Tale

Retold by Patience Clay

Illustrated by Nikki Frances Fonacier

ISBN: 978-1-954790-00-1

v1.02

Margaret Thatcher was born Margaret Roberts to a middle class family in Britain.

When she grew up, she attended school to become a scientist.

She worked for several years as a chemist.

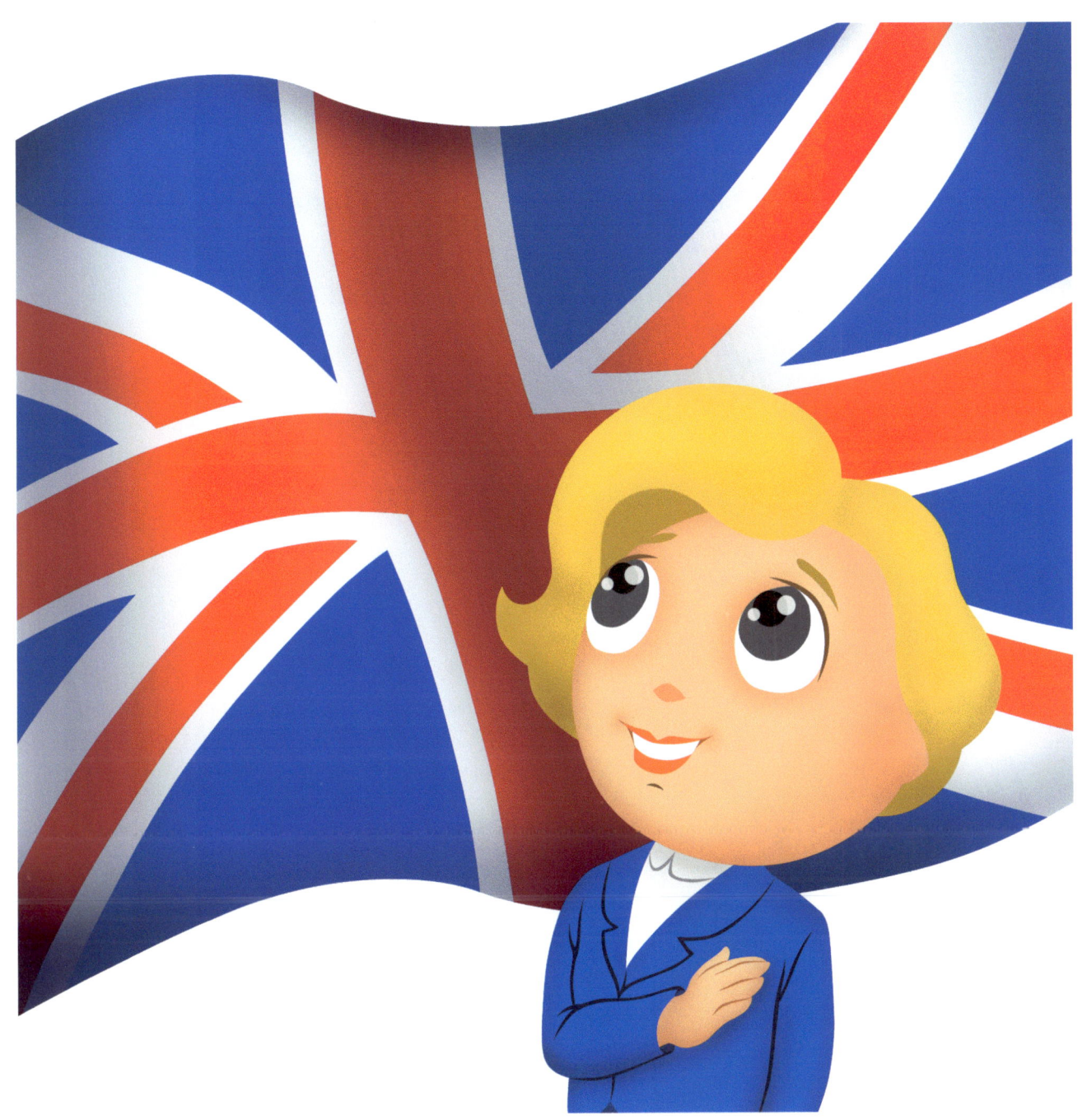

But soon, she left scientific work to enter politics.

Her talent was quickly recognized. When she was still in her 20s, people wondered if she would be Prime Minister one day.

In government, she recognized that her most important mission was to
stop Communism from spreading to the United Kingdom.

She opposed Communism by supporting free markets, free enterprise,

personal freedoms like gay rights, and a strong defense.

She proved a fierce opponent to the Soviet Union.

The Soviets tried to deride her as the "Iron Lady," but Thatcher wore the nickname proudly as a badge of strength.

She knew that lower taxes and a stronger economy would help the country grow and defeat Communism.

"There is no such thing as public money," she said, "only taxpayers' money."

Soon, she was made Prime Minister, the leader of the British government.

As Prime Minister, she continued her push for freedom. She closed unprofitable mines owned by the government...

… and sold many government-owned businesses to private owners, including members of the public who bought shares.

Some changes were unpopular at first…

…but when she was done, the people of the UK were almost twice as rich as they had been when she started.

When the UK and US won the Cold War, Thatcher was one of the first leaders to begin working with their former opponents.

1979-1990

Margaret Thatcher was Prime Minister for 21 years - the longest-serving Prime Minister of the United Kingdom ever.

She helped defeat Communism and paved the way for the United Kingdom to be the wealthy, modern country it is today.

About the Author

Patience Clay is a parent and history buff. She has always loved sharing history with her kids. Now, she wants to share some her favorite true tales with other children around the world.

Collect these other great Copper Jungle titles!

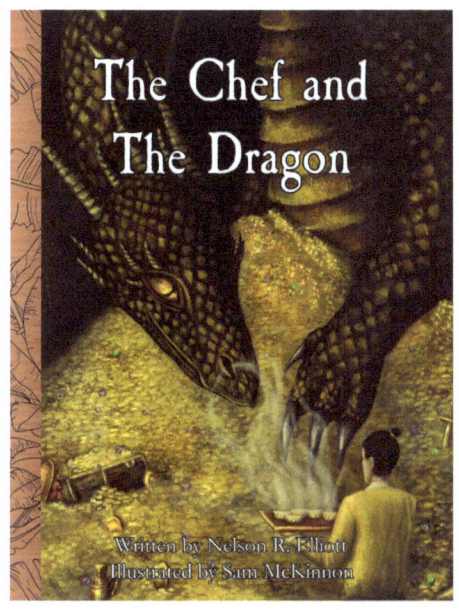

The Chef and The Dragon

Written by Nelson R. Elliott
Illustrated by Sam McKinnon

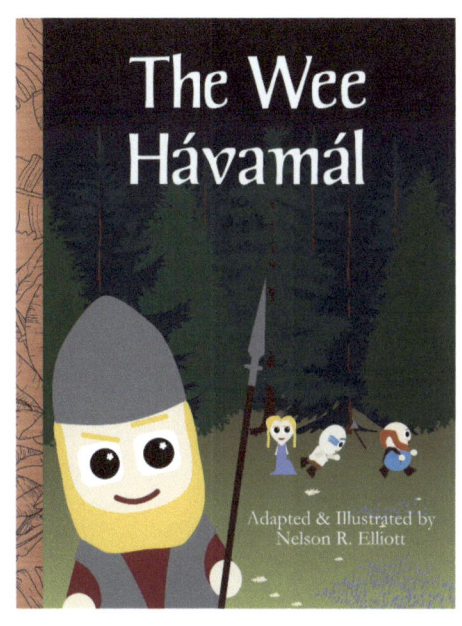

The Wee Hávamál

Adapted & Illustrated by
Nelson R. Elliott

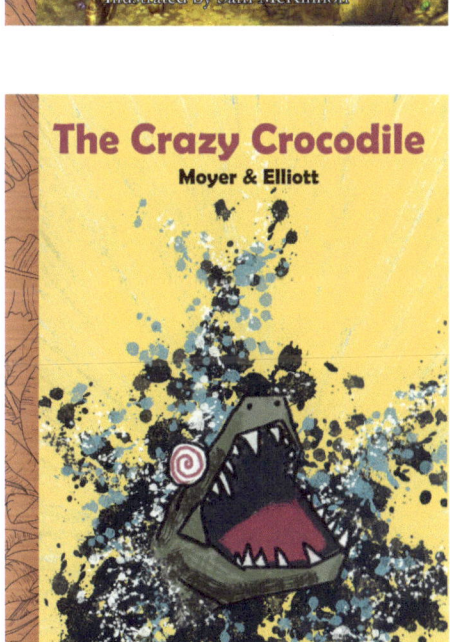

The Crazy Crocodile

Moyer & Elliott

The Lost Crow

Written by Nelson R. Elliott
Illustrated by Sam McKinnon